SO-DUS-601

To our little big teen ager Granddaughter on her 13th Birthday march 2 3–1983.

We Are very proud to have you for our Granddaughter and we do Love you very very much.

may you have many many more Happy Birthday days, and always be the sweet little girl you are today

All our Love, nanny & paw paw

Published by
Lion Publishing, Icknield Way, Tring, Herts,
England

ISBN 0–915684–70–5
Library of Congress Catalog Card No.
80–65438

First US edition 1980, published by Christian
Herald Books, Chappaqua, New York 10514

Photographs by Fritz Fankhauser: pages 12,
14, 26, 35, 36; Fisons Fertilizer Division: page
24 and endpapers; Sonia Halliday
Photographs: F. H. C. Birch, page 39 and
cover, Sonia Halliday, pages 9, 16, 23, 28, 30,
41, Jane Taylor, 7, 32, 44; Alan Hutchison
Library: page 19, Robin Constable, page 21;
Lion Publishing: David Alexander, page 10,
Jon Willcocks, page 42

Quotations from *The Holy Bible, New
International Version,* copyright 1978 New York
International Bible Society

Printed in Singapore by Tien Wah Press (PTE)
Ltd

PRAYERS
OF
JESUS

Christian Herald Books
40 Overlook Drive, Chappaqua, New York 10514

Man of prayer

Crowds of people came to hear him
and to be healed of their sicknesses.
But Jesus often withdrew to lonely
places and prayed.

Luke 5:15–16

The hills of Galilee, where Jesus often prayed.

Our Father

Seeing Jesus pray, his disciples asked him to teach them how to pray. He gave them the pattern prayer which Christians have used down the centuries.

Our Father in heaven,
hallowed be your name.

God's will,
on earth

Your kingdom come,
your will be done

on earth as it is in heaven.

The village of Maloula in Syria.

All we need

Give us today our daily bread.

Forgiveness

Forgive us our debts,
as we also have forgiven our debtors.
And lead us not into temptation,
but deliver us from the evil one.

Matthew 6:9–13

Jesus
gives thanks

When he was faced with five thousand hungry people, and only five loaves and two fish to feed them with, Jesus remained unperturbed. Calmly, as his custom was, he gave God thanks for the food provided.

Taking the five loaves and the two fish and looking up to heaven, he gave thanks and broke the loaves. Then he gave them to his disciples to set before the people. He also divided the two fish among them all. They all ate and were satisfied.

Mark 6:41–42

Jesus fed the crowds on a hillside in Galilee.

Jesus rejoices

Jesus sent out seventy-two of his followers. They were to go ahead of him, two by two, to every town and place where he was about to go. They were to heal the sick and tell people of God's kingdom: that Jesus had come to begin a new age.
The seventy-two returned with joy, telling how even the demons submitted to them in Christ's name. Jesus shared their joy, praising God:

I praise you, Father, Lord of heaven and earth, because you have hidden these things from the wise and learned, and revealed them to little children. Yes, Father, for this was your good pleasure.

Luke 10:21

Jesus blesses
the children

People brought their children to Jesus, wanting him to ask God's blessing on them. When the disciples tried to protect him from their demands, turning people away, Jesus was angry.

'Let the little children come to me, and do not hinder them, for the kingdom of God belongs to such as these. I tell you the truth, anyone who will not receive the kingdom of God like a little child will never enter it.' And he took the children in his arms, put his hands on them and blessed them.

Mark 10:14–16

Lazarus lives

Jesus' friend Lazarus had died. His sisters could not understand why Jesus had not arrived in time to heal him. They had not yet learned that his power extends beyond the grave. Jesus ordered the people to take away the stone that sealed the entrance to the tomb. Then he prayed to God.

'Father, I thank you that you have heard me. I knew that you always hear me, but I said this for the benefit of the people standing here, that they may believe that you sent me.'
When he had said this, Jesus called in a loud voice, 'Lazarus, come out!' The dead man came out, his hands and feet wrapped with strips of linen, and a cloth around his face.
Jesus said to them, 'Take off the grave clothes and let him go.'

John 11:41–44

Facing death

Jesus had been speaking to his followers about his coming death. It was necessary for him to die – just as corn must fall to the ground and die to produce new grain. Yet it was hard to face suffering.

Now my heart is troubled, and what shall I say? 'Father, save me from this hour'? No, it was for this very reason I came to this hour. Father, glorify your name!

John 12:27–28

Eternal life

On the eve of his death, in the upper room with the little group of his close friends, Jesus prayed – for himself, for his friends and for all who would believe in him.

Father, the time has come. Glorify your Son, that your Son may glorify you. For you granted him authority over all people that he might give eternal life to all those you have given him. Now this is eternal life: that they may know you, the only true God, and Jesus Christ, whom you have sent.

John 17:1–3

Houses built in traditional style, in a village in Israel.

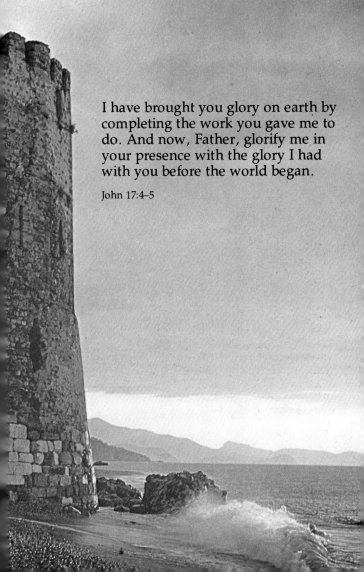

The finished work

I have brought you glory on earth by completing the work you gave me to do. And now, Father, glorify me in your presence with the glory I had with you before the world began.

John 17:4–5

All one

I am not praying for the world, but for
those you have given me, for they are
yours. All I have is yours, and all you
have is mine. And glory has come to
me through them. I will remain in the
world no longer, but they are still in

the world, and I am coming to you.
Holy Father, protect them by the
power of your name – the name you
gave me – so that they may be one as
we are one.

John 17:9–11

Women gathering olives in Tunisia.

Kept safe

My prayer is not that you take them
out of the world but that you protect
them from the evil one. They are not
of the world, even as I am not of it.
Sanctify them by the truth; your word
is truth. As you sent me into the
world, I have sent them into the
world.

John 17:15–18

A crowded street in the old city of Jerusalem.

Gethsemane

On the night of his betrayal, Jesus took his friends to a quiet orchard of olive-trees. In great agony of mind, he prayed – about the cup of suffering he was about to drink, the death he was about to die. For he was to take onto his own shoulders the burden of the world's sin.

My Father, if it is possible, may this cup be taken from me. Yet not as I will, but as you will.

Matthew 26:39

An ancient olive-tree in the Garden of Gethsemane.

Forgive them

Outside the city of Jerusalem, at the place called The Skull, Jesus was crucified, between two criminals. At the point of death he prayed for his enemies.

Father, forgive them, for they do not know what they are doing.

Luke 23:34

The Golden Gate and city walls, Jerusalem.

Alone

On the cross, Jesus took on himself the weight of human sin, the horror of separation from God the Father. He cried out in an agony of pain and loneliness.

My God, my God, why have you forsaken me?

Matthew 27:46

Last words

Jesus' dying breath, as he hung on the cross, was a prayer to God.

Father, into your hands I commit my spirit.

Luke 23:46

The risen Christ

Two days later, on the first Easter Sunday, two of Jesus' disciples were walking along a road talking of Jesus' death and the rumour that he was alive again. A stranger joined them, and as they reached the village was invited to stay. It was as he thanked God for the evening meal that they realized he was Jesus.

When he was at the table with them, he took bread, gave thanks, broke it and began to give it to them. Then their eyes were opened and they recognized him.

Luke 24:30–31

The ascension

Jesus appeared to his disciples over a period of forty days after his resurrection. When the time came for him to return to his Father, his last action was to pray God's blessing on them all.

When he had led them out to the vicinity of Bethany, he lifted up his hands and blessed them. While he was blessing them, he left them and was taken up into heaven.

Luke 24:50–51

The village of Bethany, close to Jerusalem.